中国法院知识产权
司法保护状况

2016年

Intellectual Property Protection by
Chinese Courts in 2016

人民法院出版社

图书在版编目（CIP）数据

中国法院知识产权司法保护状况（2016年）/最高人民法院知识产权审判庭编． —北京：人民法院出版社，2017．4
ISBN 978-7-5109-1802-5

Ⅰ.①中… Ⅱ.①最… Ⅲ.①知识产权保护–研究–中国–2016 Ⅳ.①D923．404

中国版本图书馆CIP数据核字（2017）第070931号

中国法院知识产权司法保护状况（2016年）

最高人民法院知识产权审判庭　编

责任编辑	丁丽娜
出版发行	人民法院出版社
地　　址	北京市东城区东交民巷27号（100745）
电　　话	（010）67550608（责任编辑）　67550558（发行部查询） 　　　　　65223677（读者服务部）
客 服 QQ	2092078039
网　　址	http://www.courtbook.com.cn
E – mail	courtpress@sohu.com
印　　刷	北京瑞禾彩色印刷有限公司
经　　销	新华书店
开　　本	787×1092毫米　1/16
字　　数	50千字
印　　张	4.5
版　　次	2017年4月第1版　2017年4月第1次印刷
书　　号	ISBN 978-7-5109-1802-5
定　　价	18.00元

版权所有　侵权必究

目 录

前言 ·· 1

一、发挥审判职能，公正高效审理知识产权案件················ 2
二、推进司法改革，科学完善知识产权审判体系················ 9
三、强化监督指导，切实保障司法裁判标准统一················ 12
四、落实司法公开，营造良好司法保护法治环境················ 16
五、加强队伍建设，全面提升司法审判队伍素质················ 18

结束语 ·· 20

附件：2016年全国法院新收知识产权案件类型与数量图 ········ 22

Content

Introduction 26

I. Performing adjudication duties to ensure fair and
    efficient adjudication 28
II. Advancing judicial reform to improve the
    adjudication system.................................... 40
III. Strengthening supervision and guidance to
    unify standards for judicial decisions............ 47
IV. Implementing open justice to create a law-based
    environment that conduces to judicial protection 54
V. Strengthening people development to improve
    the overall quality of the adjudication team 59

Conclusion 63

特别说明：

《中国法院知识产权司法保护状况（2016年）》以中英两种文本发布，以中文文本为准。

Special Remarks:

This paper is published in both Chinese and English. The Chinese version shall be the authoritative version for interpretation purposes.

中国法院知识产权司法保护状况
（2016年）

前言

2016年，人民法院在以习近平同志为核心的党中央坚强领导下，在各级人民代表大会有力监督下，全面贯彻党的十八大和十八届三中、四中、五中、六中全会、中央政法工作会议和全国科技创新大会精神，深入学习贯彻习近平总书记系列重要讲话精神和治国理政新理念新思想新战略，牢固树立"四个意识"，切实贯彻实施国家知识产权战略和国家创新驱动发展战略，紧紧围绕"努力让人民群众在每一个司法案件中感受到公平正义"目标，忠实履行宪法和法律赋予的审判职责，全面实施"司法主导、严格保护、分类施策、比例协调"知识产权司法保护基本政策，以执法办案为重心，积极发挥司法保护知识产权主导作用，深化知识产权审判体制改革，加强审判监督指导，深入推进司法公开，着力打造审判队伍建设，充分展示人民法院知识产权司法保护的良好形象，为服务国家创新发展大局，建设知识产权强国和世界科技强国提供了有力的司法保障。

一、发挥审判职能，公正高效审理知识产权案件

习近平总书记在全国科技创新大会上提出到新中国成立 100 年时使我国成为世界科技强国的伟大目标。要实现这一目标，归根到底要依靠创新驱动，推动新技术、新产业、新业态蓬勃发展。完善的知识产权保护制度是激发创新原动力的基本保障，而司法一直都是保护知识产权最有效、最根本、最权威的手段。一年来，人民法院充分发挥司法保护知识产权的主导作用，以民事审判为基础，行政审判和刑事审判并行发展，公正高效地审理了大量知识产权案件。2016 年，人民法院共新收一审、二审、申请再审等各类知识产权案件 177705 件，审结 171708 件（含旧存，下同），比 2015 年分别上升 19.07% 和 20.86%。

（一）妥善审理知识产权民事案件，维护权利人合法权益

一年来，人民法院加强知识产权民事审判工作，严格保护知识产权，给权利人提供充分的司法救济。2016 年，地方各级人民法院共新收和审结知识产权民事一审案件 136534 件和 131813 件，分别比 2015 年上升 24.82% 和 30.09%，一审结案率为 83.18%，同比上升 0.52%。其中，新收专利案件 12357 件，同比上升 6.46%；商标案件 27185 件，同比上升 12.48%；著作权案件 86989 件，同比上升 30.44%；技术合同案件 2401 件，同比上升 62.23%；竞争类案件

2286 件（含垄断民事案件 156 件），同比上升 4.81%；其他知识产权民事纠纷案件 5316 件，同比上升 71.87%。全年共审结涉外知识产权民事一审案件 1667 件，同比上升 25.62%；审结涉港澳台知识产权民事一审案件 1130 件，同比上升 291.99%。地方各级人民法院共新收和审结知识产权民事二审案件 20793 件和 20334 件，同比分别上升 37.57% 和 35.33%；共新收和审结知识产权民事再审案件 79 件和 85 件，同比分别下降 31.30% 和 25.44%。

2016 年，最高人民法院新收知识产权民事案件 369 件，审结 383 件，新收和审结与去年同比基本持平。其中，新收和审结二审案件 7 件和 11 件；新收和审结申请再审案件 319 件和 331 件；新收提审案件 32 件，审结 32 件。

一年来，人民法院审结的具有较大社会影响的知识产权民事案件有：礼来公司诉常州华生制药有限公司侵害发明专利权纠纷案；松下电器产业株式会社与珠海金稻电器有限公司、北京丽康富雅商贸有限公司侵害外观设计专利权纠纷案；上海晨光文具股份有限公司与得力集团有限公司、济南坤森商贸有限公司侵害外观设计专利权纠纷案；北京庆丰包子铺与山东庆丰餐饮管理有限公司侵害商标权与不正当竞争纠纷再审案；江苏省广播电视总台、深圳市珍爱网信息技术有限公司与金阿欢侵害商标权纠纷再审案；杭州大头儿子文化发展有限公司与央视动画有限公司侵害著作权纠纷案；河北省林业科学研究院、石家庄市绿缘达园林工程有限公司与九台市园林绿化管理处等侵害植物新品种权纠纷再审案等。

（二）妥善审理知识产权行政案件，发挥监督促进职能作用

人民法院按照建设社会主义法治国家的目标，严格适用新修订的行政诉讼法，充分发挥司法对知识产权授权确权和行政执法行为的监督作用，严格规范知识产权行政执法行为，积极促进行政机关依法行政。2016年，地方各级人民法院共新收知识产权行政一审案件7186件，其中，专利案件1123件，商标案件5990件，著作权案件37件，其他行政案件36件。审结一审案件6250件，其中，涉外、涉港澳台案件2394件，占38.30%。在审结的一审案件中，判决维持具体行政行为的4241件，判决撤销的1263件。地方各级人民法院新收知识产权行政二审案件3233件，审结3069件，同比分别上升44%和31.77%。其中，维持原判2560件，改判418件，发回重审7件，撤诉49件，驳回20件，以其他方式结案15件。

2016年，最高人民法院新收和审结知识产权行政案件355件和352件，与去年基本持平。其中，新收申请再审案件282件，审结283件。

一年来，人民法院审结的具有较大社会影响的知识产权行政案件有：迈克尔·杰弗里·乔丹与国家工商行政管理总局商标评审委员会、乔丹体育股份有限公司商标争议行政纠纷再审案；国家知识产权局专利复审委员会、诺维信公司与江苏博立生物制品有限公司发明专利权无效行政纠纷再审案；拉菲罗斯柴尔德酒庄与国家工商行政管理总局商标评审委员会、南京金色希望酒业有限公司商标争议行政纠纷再审案等。

（三）妥善审理知识产权刑事案件，惩治侵犯知识产权犯罪

一年来，人民法院坚持宽严相济刑事政策，依法运用各种刑事制裁措施，严厉惩治和震慑侵犯知识产权犯罪，保护权利人合法权益，维护合法有序的社会经济秩序。2016年，地方各级人民法院共新收涉知识产权刑事一审案件8352件，同比下降23.9%。其中，侵犯知识产权罪案件3799件（侵犯注册商标犯罪案件3565件，侵犯著作权罪案件195件），同比下降22.67%；涉及侵犯知识产权的生产、销售伪劣商品罪案件2765件，同比下降29.55%；涉及侵犯知识产权的非法经营罪案件1567件，同比下降18.51%；涉及侵犯知识产权的其他案件221件，同比上升3.27%。

地方各级人民法院共审结涉知识产权刑事一审案件8601件，同比下降20.43%，一审结案率为89.06%，同比基本持平；生效判决人数10431人，同比下降18.13%；给予刑事处罚10334人，同比下降17.85%。其中，审结侵犯知识产权罪案件3903件，生效判决人数5167人；涉及侵犯知识产权的生产、销售伪劣商品罪案件2855件，生效判决人数3032人；涉及侵犯知识产权的非法经营罪案件1551件，生效判决人数1790人；涉及侵犯知识产权的其他罪名案件292件，生效判决人数442人。在审结的侵犯知识产权罪案件中，假冒注册商标罪案件1793件，生效判决人数2604人；销售假冒注册商标的商品罪案件1543件，生效判决人数1823人；非法制造、销售非法制造的注册商标标识罪案件311件，生效判决人数420人；假冒专利罪案件5件，生效判决人数1人；侵犯著作权罪案件207件，生效判决人数274人；销售侵权复制品罪案件4件，生效判决人数2人；

侵犯商业秘密罪案件 40 件，生效判决人数 43 人。

地方各级人民法院共新收涉知识产权的刑事二审案件 787 件，同比基本持平；审结 812 件，同比上升 3.83%。

一年来，人民法院审结的具有较大社会影响的知识产权刑事案件有：汪紫平侵犯商业秘密犯罪案；沈靓等假冒注册商标等犯罪案；邓丰成、程先荣等假冒注册商标和销售假冒注册商标的商品犯罪案；彭梵侵犯商业秘密犯罪案。

2016 年，人民法院知识产权案件审判工作呈现出下列四个新特点：

案件数量再创新高。 2016 年，人民法院新收知识产权民事、行政和刑事案件数量大幅增加，其中，一审案件 152072 件，比 2015 年上升 16.80%。知识产权民事一审案件上升幅度最为明显，达到 24.82%。北京、上海、江苏、浙江、广东五省市法院收案数量一直保持高位运行态势，新收各类知识产权案件数合计 107011 件，占全国法院的 70.37%。其中，广东法院收案数量同比上升 22.36%，上海法院收案数量同比上升 20.74%。山东、福建法院新收各类知识产权案件同比增幅也均在 20% 以上。其他一些省份法院也一改往年案件数量偏少的状况，如贵州法院随着工业强省、城镇化带动战略的推进，案件数量增长迅猛，同比上升了 58.20%。重庆法院的知识产权案件数量也大幅攀升，全年新收知识产权案件同比上升 57.85%。湖南、安徽法院知识产权一审案件数量也增长迅速，分别同比上升 52.02% 和 45.4%。

审理难度逐步增大。 知识产权案件尤其是技术类案件涉及复杂技术事实认定，案件审理难度大。一年来，涉及高精尖技术的专利案件，涉及新技术合作开发、技术成果应用纠纷等技术类案件明显增多，无疑增加了事实查明和分析判断的难度。2016年，山东法院技术合同案件收案同比上升119%；上海知识产权法院审结的一审案件中，涉及专利、计算机软件、技术秘密等技术类案件占95%以上。北京法院审结的"含核苷酸类似物的复合物或盐及其合成方法"发明专利权无效行政纠纷案涉及马库什权利要求等复杂的医药化学问题。除了技术类案件以外，一些商标纠纷案件由于涉及知名品牌利益保护，一些著作权纠纷案件涉及互联网新技术，一些垄断及不正当竞争纠纷涉及市场竞争秩序维护，社会关注度高，案件事实复杂难辨，法律适用新奇特殊，使知识产权审判不断面临新挑战。如北京法院审理的"枭龙"商标行政纠纷案涉及枭龙战机；腾讯公司"宫锁连城"作品纠纷案涉及信息网络传播权解释；奇虎诉百度不正当竞争纠纷案涉及robots协议；等等。

审判质效稳中向好。一是再审率大幅下降。2016年，地方各级人民法院审结的知识产权民事一审案件虽然同比上升30.09%，但是二审案件的改判发回重审率为5.94%，与上一年基本持平，再审率同比下降45%。知识产权行政二审案件的改判发回重审率为13.85%，同比下降1.56%。二是案件调撤率大幅上升。地方各级人民法院民事一审案件调解撤诉率达到64.21%，二审案件调解撤诉率达到27.44%，取得了良好的法律效果和社会效果。上海法院知识产权民事案件调撤率达到73.92%；山东法院知识产权民事一审案件调撤率达到69.70%。天津三级法院上下联动，积极发挥司法能动性，在查清案件事实的基础上，圆满调解了涉齐白石作品的数百起著作权纠纷案，使双方当事人历经十余年的纠纷全部得以化解。江西法院创新调解方式，引导 20 多家文化传媒公司与集体管理组织签订著作权许可使用合同，化解了社会矛盾，规范了版权市场秩序，降低了社会成本。三是结案数量大幅上升。重庆法院审结一、二审知识产权案件同比上升 62.74%；湖南法院审结知识产权一审案件同比上升 48.79%；广东法院审结知识产权民事案件同比上升 42.82%；江苏法院审结知识产权民事一审案件同比上升 30.8%。

赔偿力度有所提升。人民法院逐步探索将市场价值作为知识产权赔偿数额计算的参考，依法加大对关键核心技术和知名品牌的保护力度。通过对律师费等诉讼合理支出在赔偿额中单独计算和推进适用惩罚性赔偿等措施，使赔偿数额与知识产权市场价值相适应。北京市高级人民法院审结的松下电器产业株式会社与珠海金稻电器有限公司、北京丽康富雅商贸有限公司侵害外观设计专利权纠纷案，全额支持松下株式会社 300 万元的赔偿请求。北京知识产权法院在"紫玉"商标侵权上诉案、书生公司系列侵犯著作权上诉案中，也全额支持权利人的赔偿额请求。与此同时，严厉惩处诉讼不诚信行为，对提供伪证、虚假陈述、故意逾期举证、毁损证据、妨碍证人作证等不诚信诉讼行为，依法给予程序和实体制裁。北京市高级人民法院在青岛科尼乐机械公司专利侵权案中，对拒不履行法院生效保全裁定的当事人处以 50 万元的罚款。

二、推进司法改革，科学完善知识产权审判体系

2016年是"十三五"规划的开局之年，也是人民法院全面深化司法体制改革的攻坚之年。人民法院锐意改革、勇于创新、精准发力、定向施策，积极推进知识产权司法体制机制改革，推动知识产权司法保护体系和能力向现代化迈进。

（一）大力推进知识产权法院建设

2016年，北京、上海、广州知识产权法院各项工作有序开展，司法职能有效发挥，全体法官凝心聚力，依托司法科技创新和制度创新，努力推进专业化、精细化、法治化建设，改革成效和标杆作用逐步显现，司法公信力和国际影响力持续增强，展示了中国知识产权司法保护的新形象。知识产权法院率先进行司法改革，形成院、庭长办案常态化机制，转变审判委员会职能，探索审判委员会参加案件审理的方式，成效良好。2016年，三家知识产权法院共受理知识产权民事和行政案件17268件，审结14896件，结案率达86.26%。北京知识产权法院大力推进案例指导研究（北京）基地建设工作，上海知识产权法院积极服务上海科技创新中心建设，广州知识产权法院大力加强知识产权市场化研究，树立了中国法院知识产权审判的新形象。最高人民法院知识产权审判庭深入调查研究知识产权法院在改革发展中遇到的困难和问题，撰写完成《知识产权法院设立及工作情况》，积极推进"知识产权法院建立重大问题研究"课题项目的调研工作，为建立知识产权上诉机制提供实践指引。

（二）全面深入推进"三合一"改革工作

2016 年，知识产权审判"三合一"工作取得重大进展与突破。除知识产权法院暂不执行"三合一"以外，"三合一"工作在全国法院全面推开。7 月 5 日，《最高人民法院关于在全国法院推进知识产权民事、行政和刑事案件审判"三合一"工作的意见》印发。7 月 7 日，最高人民法院在江苏省南京市召开全国法院知识产权审判工作会议暨全国法院推进知识产权审判"三合一"工作会议，全面部署推进"三合一"工作，"三合一"工作迈上新台阶。目前，最高人民法院正在与有关部门就知识产权刑事司法实施方案进行积极沟通，以期尽快会签相关文件，全面推进"三合一"工作，提高知识产权司法保护的整体效能。

（三）筹划设立知识产权专门审判机构

最高人民法院知识产权审判庭拟定在南京、苏州、武汉、成都等地设立知识产权专门审判机构及其案件管辖的具体方案。2017 年年初，上述四个专门审判机构相继挂牌，开始受理案件。南京知识产权法庭、苏州知识产权法庭分别以南京中院和苏州中院知识产权庭为基础组建，按独立机构模式运行，在省内分别跨区域管辖专利等技术类知识产权一审民事案件等。武汉知识产权审判庭实行"三合一"，除管辖武汉市辖区知识产权民事、行政和刑事案件外，还跨区域管辖湖北全省有关专利等技术类一审知识产权民事和行政案件。成都知识产权审判庭跨区域管辖四川省内专利等技术类一审知识产权民事、行政案件。

（四）优化技术事实查明机制

完善的技术事实查明机制对知识产权案件公正裁判具有极其重要的作用。最高人民法院已经出台了《关于知识产权法院技术调查官参与诉讼活动若干问题的暂行规定》，正在抓紧制定知识产权法院技术调查官选任工作指导意见。上海市高级人民法院制定《关于知识产权民事诉讼中涉及技术事实司法鉴定的操作指引》，完善多元化技术事实查明机制。北京知识产权法院成立技术调查室，制定《技术调查官管理办法》。该院2016年技术类案件收结比率同比上升27.5%。广州知识产权法院从行政机关、院校、科研机构等单位聘请29名专家，组成技术专家咨询委员会，为案件审理提供专业意见。该院2016年共有88件案件启用技术专家或技术调查官，案件调撤率达64.7%。贵州省高级人民法院与贵州省科技厅合作，聘请科学技术咨询专家，为案件中涉及的专门性技术问题提供咨询意见以查清技术事实。四川省高级人民法院遴选电子信息技术、机械制造、医药、植物新品种等领域的专家进入知识产权技术专家库，丰富技术事实认定体系。

（五）健全多元化纠纷解决机制

近年来，人民法院的知识产权案件呈现逐年增多的趋势，"案多人少"的矛盾日益突出。因此,健全和加强多元化纠纷解决机制建设，对提高知识产权司法质量和效率具有重要的现实意义。北京法院加强与北京市保护知识产权举报投诉服务中心、中国互联网协会调解中心等相关单位的对接，充分调动行政调解、行业调解、人民调解组织的力量，推进纠纷的和解解决。上海知识产权法院与中国互联网协会调解中心、上海市软件行业协会、上海市生物医药行业协会、上海市工商联民商事人民调解委员会、东方公证处等10家社会组织和机构建立诉讼与非诉讼相衔接的多元化纠纷解决合作机制，推进诉前调解、诉调对接，形成优势互补、资源共享的多元化纠纷解决机制。去年一年，该院经双方当事人同意进入诉前调解的案件有96件，调解成功23件。福建法院注重发挥行业协会和科技专家的专业技术优势，实施委托调解、行业调解、科技专家调解，发挥协同解决知识产权纠纷作用，公正、有效地解决了一大批案件。

三、强化监督指导，切实保障司法裁判标准统一

统一司法裁判标准是提升司法公信力，树立司法权威的重要手段。2016年，人民法院继续加强司法解释和司法政策的制定工作，完善审判监督和审判管理工作机制，不断提高知识产权审判工作水平，确保司法裁判标准的统一。

（一）加强司法解释和司法政策的制定工作

制定《最高人民法院关于审理侵害专利权纠纷案件应用法律若干问题的解释（二）》。该解释由最高人民法院审判委员会于2016年1月25日通过，自2016年4月1日起施行。该解释进一步完善了专利侵权判定规则，明确权利要求的选择、权利要求解释、近似外观设计、间接侵权、抵触申请抗辩、标准实施抗辩、生产经营目的、合法来源抗辩、赔偿数额的计算、专利法第四十七条的适用等法律应用问题，有效促进专利法的正确适用。

制定《最高人民法院关于审理商标授权确权行政案件若干问题的规定》。该规定由最高人民法院审判委员会于 2016 年 12 月 12 日通过，自 2017 年 3 月 1 日起施行。该规定针对司法实践中存在的突出问题，在 2010 年发布的《关于审理商标授权确权行政案件若干问题的意见》基础上制定，主要涉及审查范围、显著特征判断、驰名商标保护、著作权及姓名权等在先权利保护等实体内容，以及违反法定程序、一事不再理等程序内容，对商标授权确权行政案件所涉及的重要问题和审判实践中的难点问题进行了明确。该规定是最高人民法院总结审判实践经验、完善商标授权确权法律适用标准的重要举措，对倡导诚实信用理念、形成良好的商标申请和注册秩序、统一裁判标准具有重要意义。

制定《中国知识产权司法保护纲要 2016—2020》。该纲要共分为前言、成就回顾、指导思想、基本原则、主要目标、重点措施和结束语七个部分，为未来五年人民法院知识产权司法保护明确指导思想和目标，确定保护原则和措施，规划发展路径和蓝图。该纲要着力补齐短板，提出了知识产权司法保护的努力方向和解决方案，从根本上破解司法保护良性发展的瓶颈问题。该纲要是最高人民法院第一次就专门审判领域制定发布保护纲要，是最高人民法院贯彻落实中央精神的具体举措，是加强产权保护和将经济发展新理念融入知识产权司法保护工作中的集中体现，是贯彻落实习近平总书记系列重要讲话精神和治国理政新理念新思路新战略，指导知识产权司法保护实践的重要成果。该纲要于 2017 年"4·26"期间发布。

此外，最高人民法院正在抓紧研究《最高人民法院关于审查知识产权与竞争纠纷行为保全案件适用法律若干问题的解释》《最高人民法院关于充分发挥司法保护知识产权主导作用加快知识产权强国建设若干问题的意见》，通过完善司法解释和司法政策更好地监督指导全国知识产权司法保护工作。

（二）加强审判指导和审判调研工作

推动法律编纂修订工作。 积极参与民法典、专利法、著作权法、反不正当竞争法、种子法、商标法实施条例等法律法规的编纂修订工作，提出修改意见并建议将知识产权纳入民法典。最高人民法院专门成立跨部门专利法修改调研小组，积极开展调研，系统总结专利法实施30年来司法实践中积累的经验，深入研究专利审判中遇到的困难和问题，向国务院法制办提出了专利法修改的总体方案以及具体条文修改意见。

加强法律适用的专题研究。 最高人民法院开展"商业模式等新形态创新成果的知识产权保护办法"专题调研工作，对审理电影作品和以类似摄制电影的方法创作的作品民事纠纷案件适用法律问题以及著作权集体管理制度的相关问题进行调研，配合全国工商联开展民营企业知识产权保护专题调研，参与"标题党"整治工作，为净化网络环境提供法律支持。北京市高级人民法院在调研的基础上形成并发布《北京市高级人民法院关于网络知识产权案件的审理指南》，针对商标、专利授权确权案件出台了审判参考问答。上海市高级人民法院就"商标多重许可中的法律问题""涉深层链接的著作权侵权问题""计算机软件专利权保护"开展调研。江苏省高级人民法院开展"供给侧结构性改革可能引发的法律问题及司法应对"调研，完成《关于侵犯商标权纠纷案件相关审理问题的调研报告》《技术创新背景下的专利案件裁判尺度》等调研报告。湖南省高级人民法院完成《知识产权案件技术事实查明机制研究》《知识产权行政保护与司法保护的冲突和协调研究》等课题。贵州省高级人民法院完成《黔茶知识产权保护问题研究——模式、问题及对策》调研报告及贵州省重点课题《非物质文化遗产保护》。吉林省高级人民法院积极开展朝医朝药调研，以推进中医药的知识产权保护。

重视与行政机关的沟通交流。最高人民法院知识产权审判庭与国家知识产权局专利复审委员会开展业务交流，进一步明确和统一专利授权确权纠纷解决的法律规则；与商标评审委员会开展业务交流，就商标保护相关法律适用问题进行深入沟通和研讨；与农业部种子局共同启动植物新品种保护司法解释修订的调研工作。北京市高级人民法院与国家工商行政管理总局商标局、商标评审委员以及国家知识产权局专利复审委员会多次召开专题研讨会，对具体法律适用问题进行研讨。内蒙古法院与文化市场行政管理部门沟通协调，尝试从源头解决涉卡拉OK经营者著作权纠纷系列案件，初步形成呼和浩特地区版权使用费的三级收费标准。

发挥案例指导作用。最高人民法院知识产权审判庭定期发布典型案例，编辑出版《知识产权审判指导》《中国知识产权指导案例评注》。筛选出北京奇虎科技有限公司诉腾讯科技（深圳）有限公司等滥用市场支配地位纠纷案等十个案例，作为最高人民法院发布的第16批指导性案例，该批案例已经于2017年3月6日发布。最高人民法院知识产权案例指导研究(北京)基地总结案例指导工作的经验，积极开展案例指导研究工作。

四、落实司法公开，营造良好司法保护法治环境

"正义不仅要实现，还要以看得见的方式实现。"2016年，人民法院全面深化司法公开，着力构建开放、动态、透明、便民的阳光司法机制，实现司法公开的转型升级，让公开更规范、更实效、更贴心、更均衡。

（一）加强司法公开，促进司法公正

努力做好重大案件的庭审公开。最高人民法院在"4·26"期间公开审理"乔丹"商标争议行政纠纷案，陶凯元副院长担任审判长，通过全媒体对案件的审理和宣判进行了直播。来自美国、欧盟、日本、韩国等国家的驻华使节以及美国全国商会代表到庭旁听了案件的庭审。新华社、中央电视台和新加坡联合早报等20余家中外媒体记者全程旁听案件审理并进行现场报道，中国法院网、最高人民法院官方微博等对案件庭审全程无缝隙直播。仅新浪法院频道全程直播累计观看人数即超过150万，覆盖人数达9800万人次。该案的审理向国内外各界人士展现了中国法院公开透明、公正司法、平等保护中外双方当事人合法权益的良好风貌。

积极做好裁判文书公开。人民法院不断完善知识产权裁判文书公开上网管理机制，对于适宜公开的裁判文书，督促将裁判文书及时上网，接受全社会的监督，以公开促公正，让人民群众切实感受到司法的公平正义。

不断推进审判流程公开。在中国审判流程信息公开网及时推送知识产权案件流程信息，保障当事人和人民群众的知情权、监督权。

（二）加强交流与合作，提升司法形象

最高人民法院以"中国知识产权司法保护国际交流（上海）基地"为平台，健全知识产权司法保护的国际和区际交流，加强与国际组织、其他国家之间的交流合作。派员参加中美法治对话、中欧知识产权对话及工作组会议、自由贸易区知识产权章节谈判以及中瑞、中美、中澳、中俄知识产权工作组会议等各类对外工作会议并提交书面意见。派员赴美国及欧洲出访，参加越南河内召开的"UPOV公约下植物育种者权利的执行"研讨会和在韩国召开的中国知识产权保护制度说明会。上海市高级人民法院成功举办"中欧法官论坛——创新驱动与知识产权司法保护"国际会议，全年接待来自十多个国家、地区及国际组织的官员、司法机构人员和企业代表。重庆市高级人民法院与西南政法大学知识产权学院共同举办多期"中国知识产权法官讲坛"。上海知识产权法院与华东政法大学、同济大学建立合作共建机制，与上海对外经贸大学和上海政法学院建立法律服务志愿者机制。

（三）拓宽宣传渠道，实现宣传常态化

最高人民法院继续开展"4·26"世界知识产权日宣传周活动，形成知识产权司法宣传常态化。组织中央媒体"知识产权司法保护浙江行"，召开媒体见面会和新闻发布会，发布《中国法院知识产权司法保护状况（2015年）》（中英文）、2015年中国法院十大知识产权案件和五十件典型知识产权案例及《最高人民法院知识产权案件年度报告（2015）》。地方各级人民法院也积极拓宽宣传渠道，富有成效地开展工作。江苏省高级人民法院在其新浪微博、微信公众号同步开设"知产视野"栏目，交流总结全省重大疑难知识产权案件的裁判经验。浙江省高级人民法院成立"浙江法院新闻网·知之汇"子网，发布全省知识产权动态等信息，网站年点击量逾19万次。广东省高级人民法院规定参与评选优秀庭审的案件均应通过网络进行直播，快播公司著作权行政处罚纠纷、"非诚勿扰"商标侵权纠纷等受到社会广泛关注的重大案件庭审均通过广东法院网进行了视频直播。上海知识产权法院开通中英文版互联网站和官方微博、公共微信平台，接受媒体专访，在新华社、中央电视台等媒体刊发稿件156篇。陕西省高级人民法院在"4·26"期间通过网络视频直播对五起社会关注度高的新型疑难和重大典型知识产权案件进行了集中公开宣判，《西安日报》和《人民法院报》相继予以报道。

五、加强队伍建设，全面提升司法审判队伍素质

队伍建设是知识产权司法保护的基础和保障。必须深刻把握党和国家工作大局对知识产权审判队伍建设提出的新要求，坚持全面从严治党，按照党中央《关于新形势下加强政法队伍建设的意见》要求，努力打造一支信念坚定、司法为民、敢于担当、清正廉洁的知识产权审判队伍。

（一）加强思想政治建设，提升政治素养

知识产权审判队伍建设始终坚持党的领导，牢固树立"四个意

识"，深入学习贯彻习近平总书记系列重要讲话精神，坚定不移走中国特色社会主义法治道路，在思想上政治上行动上始终同以习近平同志为核心的党中央保持高度一致。积极开展"两学一做"学习教育活动，注重从中华优秀传统文化中汲取道德人文素养，弘扬社会主义先进文化和人民司法优良传统，自觉践行并坚决捍卫社会主义核心价值观。

（二）加强履职能力建设，提高专业水平

提升履职能力，是知识产权司法队伍建设的重要目标。必须大力加强履职能力建设，不断提升审判专业水平，着力培养一批讲大局、懂法律、懂技术、具有国际视野的复合型知识产权法官队伍，以适应知识迅速更新、实践快速发展的新形势。最高人民法院组织全国法院知识产权法官业务培训，陶凯元副院长为学员作专题讲座。北京市高级人民法院将年度集中培训与专题讲座相结合，拓宽业务培训的渠道。北京知识产权法院发挥资深法官的传帮带作用，对青年法官进行形式多样、内容丰富的专业培训。上海市高级人民法院举办"法经济学高级研修班""法经济学·反垄断高级研修班"，提升法官理论水平和业务能力。安徽省高级人民法院将新业务规范、新审判理念列入集体学习内容，利用部门微信样拓展"八小时"以外学习平台。海南省高级人民法院提出"一条主线、两个结合、三型党支部、四种意识、五大发展、六个原则"的工作方法，使各项工作整体推进。

（三）加强司法作风建设，树立良好形象

打铁还需自身硬，队伍强则事业兴，司法廉洁建设是队伍建设的重要环节。全国法院要坚持标本兼治，深入推进党风廉政建设和反腐败斗争，坚持从严教育、从严管理、从严监督，以零容忍态度惩治司法腐败，确保司法公正廉洁。大力加强自身建设，锤炼对党忠诚的政治品格，锻造严于律己的过硬作风，从违法违纪案件中汲取教训，及时发现和纠正不正当的苗头倾向，切实做到防微杜渐。注重家庭教育，形成廉洁家风，强化亲情助廉措施，让家人当好审判队伍的"守门员"。

结束语

2017年是实施"十三五"规划的重要一年，也是深化司法体制改革的决战之年，更是知识产权司法保护大发展之年。人民法院知识产权司法保护将深入贯彻习近平总书记系列重要讲话精神和治国理政新理念新思路新战略，牢牢抓住新一轮科技革命的历史性机遇，积极主动适应国际形势新变化和经济发展新常态，牢固树立"四个意识"，按照"五位一体"总体布局和"四个全面"战略布局要求，遵循"创新、协调、绿色、开放、共享"发展理念，深入贯彻实施国家知识产权战略，积极完善产权保护制度，依法保护产权。紧紧围绕"努力让人民群众在每一个司法案件中感受到公平正义"目标，坚持司法为民、公正司法，充分发挥司法保护知识产权主导作用，加强知识产权司法保护力度，为推动国家创新驱动发展战略实施营造良好法治环境，为建设知识产权强国和世界科技强国提供坚强有力的司法保障，以优异成绩迎接中国共产党第十九次全国代表大会的胜利召开！

附件：

2016年全国法院新收知识产权案件类型与数量图

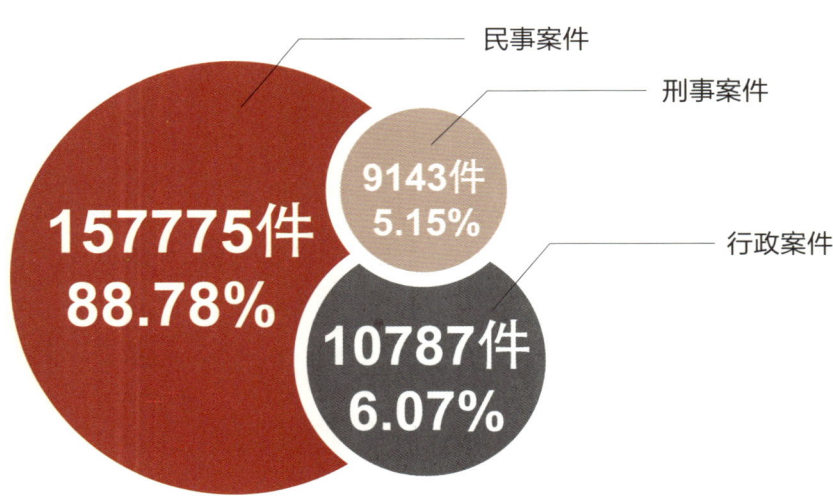

图1 2016年全国法院新收知识产权案件类型与数量图

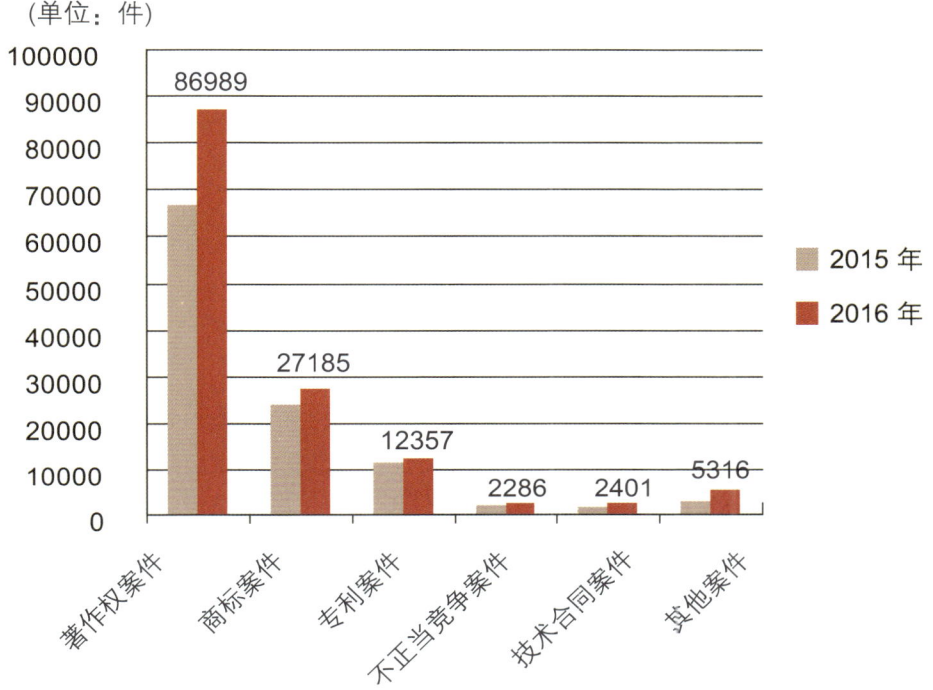

图2 2016年全国地方各级人民法院新收知识产权民事一审案件同比增幅图

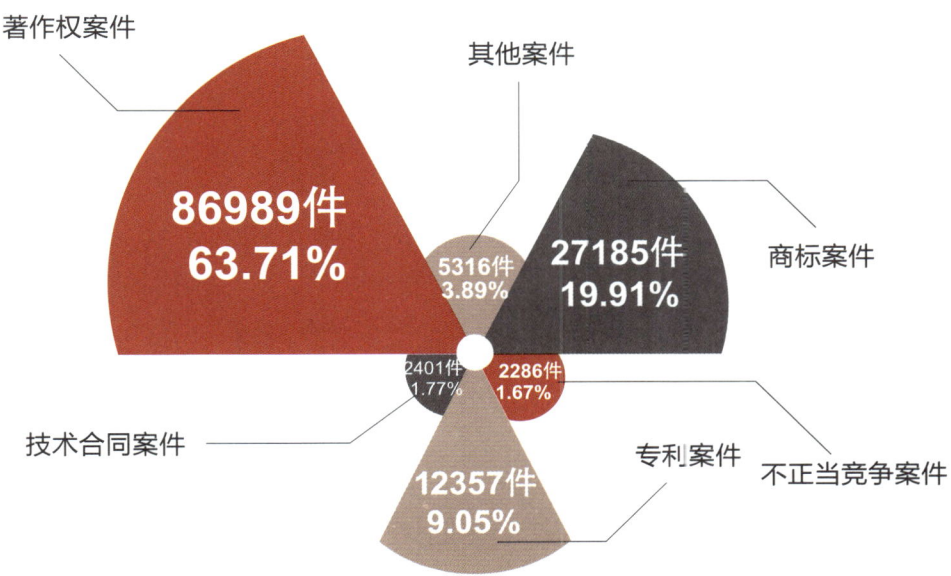

图3 2016年全国地方各级人民法院新收知识产权民事一审案件类型与数量图

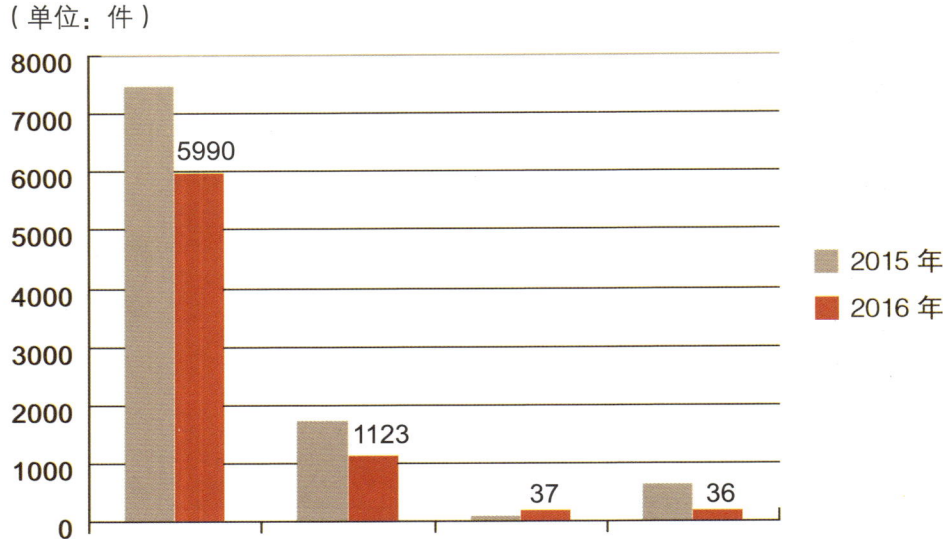

图4 2016年全国地方各级人民法院新收知识产权行政一审案件同比增幅图

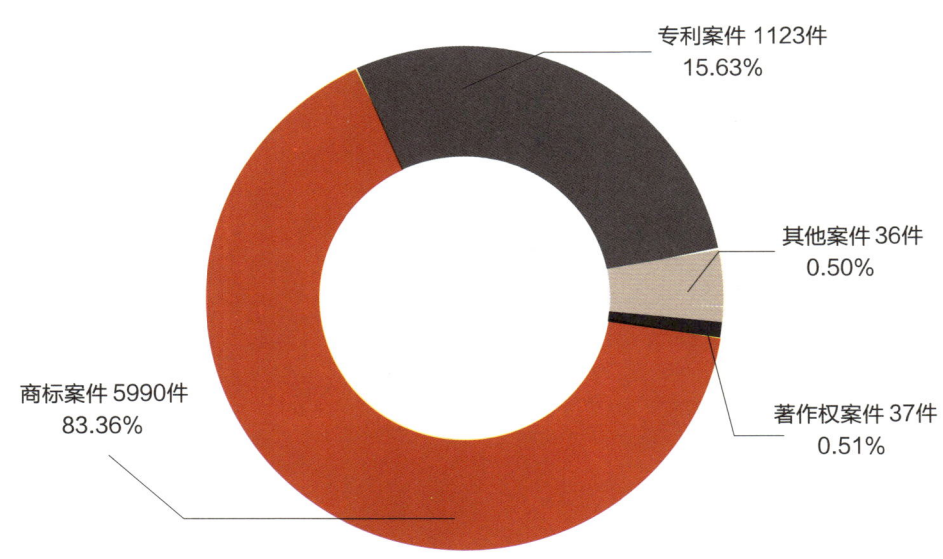

图5 2016年全国地方各级人民法院新收知识产权行政一审案件类型与数量图

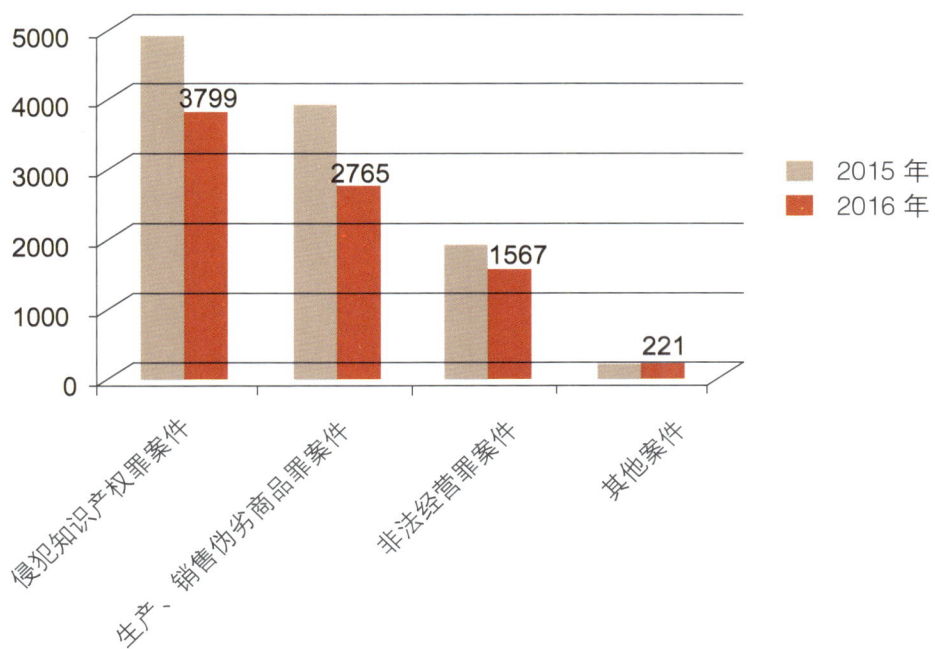

图6　2016年全国地方各级人民法院新收知识产权刑事一审案件同比增幅图

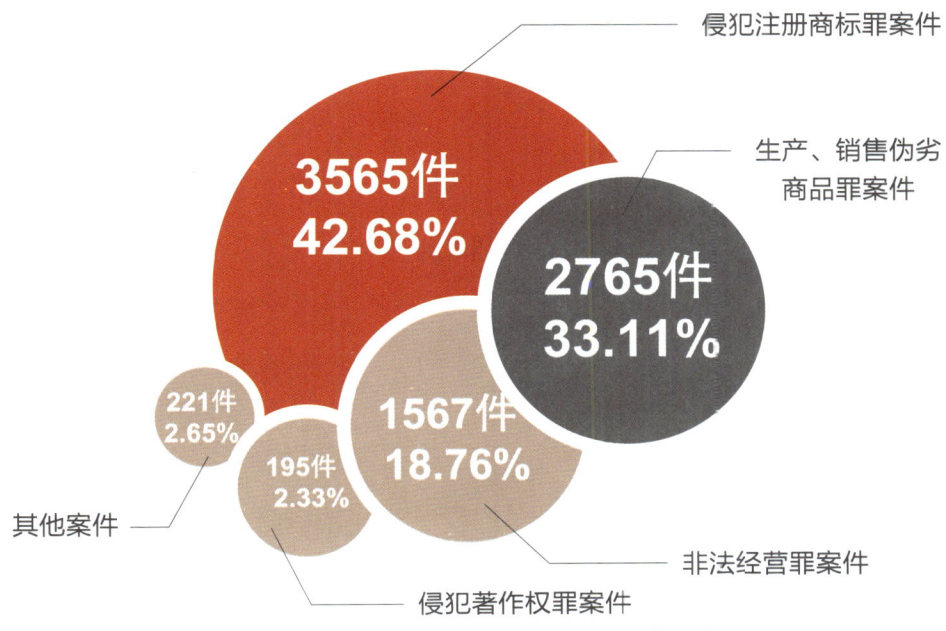

图7　2016年全国地方各级人民法院新收知识产权刑事一审案件类型与数量图

Intellectual Property Protection by Chinese Courts in 2016

Introduction

In 2016, under the strong leadership of the Communist Party of China (CPC) Central Committee with President Xi Jinping as the core of the leadership, and the effective supervision of all levels of People's Congresses, the People's Courts implemented the key tenets set forth at the 18th CPC National Congress, the Third, Fourth, Fifth and Sixth Plenums of the 18th CPC Central Committee, the Central Political and Legal Work Conference, and the National Conference on Science and Technology. The courts also studied and observed the spirit of CPC General Secretary Xi Jinping's key addresses and his new concepts, thoughts and strategies on governance.

The "four consciousness" (*sige yishi*) were cultivated in the People's Courts, in that they have strengthened their political consciousness, served the larger good, upheld the centrality of the CPC, and maintained consistency and unity. The courts have also implemented China's intellectual property strategy and innovation-driven development strategy, and worked hard to "ensure that the people perceive fairness and justice in every judicial case". They have delivered their adjudication duties as mandated by the Constitution and the laws, and increased judicial protection of intellectual property by adhering to the fundamental policies in intellectual property protection: primacy of the judiciary, strict enforcement of law, differentiated measures, and proportionality. With law enforcement and case handling being the kernel of its work, the judiciary has played a leading role in protecting intellectual property.

The people's courts have also deepened reform of the intellectual property adjudication system, strengthened adjudication supervision and guidance, improved judicial transparency, and built a highly professional pool of adjudication talents. These efforts have projected the people's courts as the reliable guardian of intellectual property, served China's innovation-driven development, and provided strong judicial safeguard in making China a global power-house of intellectual property and science and technology.

I. Performing adjudication duties to ensure fair and efficient adjudication

At the National Conference on Science and Technology, General Secretary Xi Jinping expressed China's aim to become a global power-house of science and technology by 2049, the centenary of the establishment of the People's Republic of China. To achieve this goal, it must promote innovation to spawn new technologies, new industries and new business models.

A sound intellectual property protection regime provides the fundamental assurance to unlock the motive power for innovation. In this case, the judiciary is the most effective, essential and authoritative channel for protecting intellectual property.

In 2016, the people's courts implemented a judiciary-led intellectual property protection system comprising civil, administrative and criminal adjudication capacities, and have adjudicated many intellectual property disputes fairly and efficiently.

In 2016, a total of 177,705 intellectual property-related cases were accepted, including first and second instance cases and reopened (*zaishen*) cases, and 171,708 cases were concluded (including carried over cases, ditto hereinafter). Compared to 2015, the respective increases were

19.07% and 20.86%.

(1) Effective civil adjudication to protect the lawful rights of intellectual property owners

In 2016, the people's courts have strengthened adjudication of civil intellectual property cases, enforced protection measures and ensured sufficient judicial relief to the intellectual property owners.

In 2016, the local people's courts accepted 136,534 and concluded 131,813 civil intellectual property cases of first instance, and the respective year-on-year increases were 24.82% and 30.09%; clearance rate was 83.18%, 0.52% higher than 2015. Among the accepted cases, 12,357 were patent cases, an increase of 6.46% from last year; 27,185 trademark cases, which increased by 12.48%; 86,989 copyright cases, a 30.44% increase; 2,401 technology contracts-related cases, a 62.23% increase; 2,286 unfair competition cases (including 156 monopoly cases), a 4.81% increase; and 5,316 cases involving other intellectual property disputes, a 71.87% increase; 1,667 cases were concluded, a 25.62% increase from last year. Among the concluded cases, 1,130 cases involved Hong Kong, Macau or Taiwan parties, representing a 291.99% increase from last year.

The local people's courts accepted 20,793 and concluded 20,334 civil intellectual property cases of second instance, higher than last year by 37.57% and 35.33% respectively; for reopened civil intellectual property cases, 79 were accepted and 85 concluded, lower than last year by 31.30% and 25.44% respectively.

In 2016, the Supreme People's Court accepted 369 civil intellectual property cases and concluded 383 cases, both of which were more or less the same as the previous year. 7 second instance cases were newly accepted, and 11 concluded; for reopened cases, 319 were accepted and 331concluded; 32 certiorari (*tishen*) cases were new cases and 32 were concluded.

High profile civil intellectual property cases heard by the people's courts include: *Eli Lilly and Company* (plaintiff, appellant) v. *Changzhou Watson Pharmaceuticals Co., Ltd* (defendant, appellee), an appellate case of inventive patent infringement; *Panasonic Corporation* (plaintiff, appellee) v. *Zhuhai East Kingdom Electrical Appliance Co., Ltd.* (defendant, appellant) and *Beijing Likang Fuya Trading Co., Ltd.* (defendant, appellant), an appellate case of design patent infringement; *Shanghai M&G Stationery Inc.* (plaintiff) v. *Ningbo DeLi Group Co., Ltd.* (defendant) and *Jinan Kunsen Trading Co., Ltd.* (defendant), a case of design patent infringement; *Beijing Qingfeng Steamed Dumpling Shop* (plaintiff, appellant) v. *Shandong Qingfeng Restaurant Management Co., Ltd* (defendant, appellee), a reopened case of trademark infringement and unfair competition dispute; *Jiangsu Broadcasting Corporation* (defendant, appellee) *and Shenzhen Zhen'ai Network Information Technology Co., Ltd* (defendant, appellee) *v. Jin Ahuan* (plaintiff, appellant), a reopened case of trademark infringement; *Hangzhou Datou Erzi Cultural Development Co., Ltd.* (plaintiff, appellant) *v. CCTV Animation Co., Ltd.* (defendant, appellant/appellee), a case of copyright infringement; *Hebei Academy of Forestry Science* (plaintiff, appellant/appellee) and *Shijiazhuang Lvyuanda Gardens Engineering Co., Ltd.* (plaintiff, appellant) *v. Jiutai City Gardening and Greenspace Management Division et al.* (defendant, appellee), a reopened case of new plant variety infringement.

(2) Effective administrative adjudication and better supervision and facilitation

The People's Courts worked towards the goal of developing a socialist rule of law system and applied the revised Administrative Litigation Law. Through judicial review, the courts have exercised effective oversight of granting and validation of intellectual property rights, and strictly regulated administrative law enforcement in intellectual property cases to facilitate "administering according to law (*yifa xingzheng*)".

In 2016, the local people's courts accepted 7,186 administrative intellectual property cases of first instance. Specifically, 1,123 were patent cases, 5,990 trademark cases, 37 copyright cases, and 36 other administrative cases.

In 2016, the local people's courts concluded 6,250 administrative intellectual property cases of first instance. 2,394 cases involved foreign, Hong Kong, Macau or Taiwan parties, representing 38.30% of the administrative intellectual property cases concluded at first instance. Among the concluded administrative cases of first instance, administrative decisions were affirmed in 4,241 cases, and revoked in 1,263 cases.

The local people's courts accepted 3,233 administrative intellectual property cases of second instance, and concluded 3,069, and the respective increases were 44% and 31.77%. Among the concluded cases, the judgements were affirmed in 2,560 cases and reversed in 418 cases, 7 cases were remanded for retrial (*chongshen*), 49 withdrawn, 20 dismissed, and 15 concluded through other means.

In 2016, the Supreme People's Court accepted 355 and concluded 352 administrative intellectual property cases, both numbers being nearly the same as last year. Specifically, 282 cases were reopened, and 283 concluded.

High profile administrative intellectual property cases heard by the people's courts include: *Michael Jeffrey Jordan* (plaintiff, appellant) *v. Trademark Review and Adjudication Board of State Administration for Industry and Commerce* (defendant, appellee) and *Qiaodan Sports Company, Limited* (third party), a reopened administrative case of trademark dispute; *Patent Re-examination Board of the State Intellectual Property Office* (defendant, appellant) and *Novozymes* (third party, appellant) *v. Jiangsu Boli Bio-Products Co., Ltd.* (plaintiff, appellee), a reopened administrative case of inventive patent invalidation; and *Château Lafite Rothschild* (third party) *v. Trademark Review and Adjudication Board of State Administration for Industry and Commerce* (defendant, appellee) *and Nanjing Gold Hope Wine Co., Ltd.* (plaintiff, appellant), a reopened administrative case of trademark dispute.

(3) Effective criminal adjudication to punish crimes against intellectual property

In 2016, the People's Courts followed the policy of balancing leniency and harsh penalty for criminal matters, and adopted various criminal sanctions to severely punish and deter intellectual property crimes according to law, protected the lawful rights of intellectual property owners, and maintained socioeconomic order.

In 2016, the local people's courts accepted 8,352 intellectual property-related criminal cases of first instance, 23.9% lower than last year. Among the accepted cases, 3,799 involved intellectual property infringement crime, 3,565 registered trademark infringement crime, and 195 copyright infringement crime, a 22.67% decrease from last year; 2,765 involved manufacturing and selling counterfeit or substandard goods, a decrease of 29.55% from last year; 1,567 cases were illegal business operations, a decrease of 18.51%; and 221 other cases, a 3.27% increase from last year.

The local peoples' courts concluded 8,601 intellectual property-related criminal cases of first instance, 20.43% lower than last year. Clearance rate was 89.06%, more or less the same as last year. The number of persons under effective judgements totalled 10,431, 18.13% lower than last year, of which 10,334 were given criminal penalties, a 17.85% decrease. Of the concluded cases, 3,903 cases involved intellectual property infringement crime, and the number of persons against whom judgements were effective was 5,167. Among the intellectual property infringement cases, 2,855 involved manufacturing and selling counterfeit or substandard goods, and judgements became effective against 3,032 persons; 1,551 cases were illegal business operations, and 1,790 persons were subject to effective judgements; in another 292 other criminal cases, the number of persons against whom judgements became effective were 442.

Among the concluded cases involving intellectual property infringement crime, 1,793 involved counterfeiting registered trademarks, where judgements became effective against 2,604 persons; 1,543 involved selling goods bearing counterfeit registered trademarks, where the effective judgements involved 1,823 persons; 311 were cases of illegally manufacturing or selling illegally manufactured registered trademarks, where judgment was effective against 420 persons; 5 involved counterfeiting patent, where judgment was effective against 1 person; 207 copyright infringement crime, where the effective judgements involved 274 persons; 4 cases involved selling infringing reproductions, and judgements were effective against 2 persons; and 40 were cases of trade secret infringement crime, and 43 persons were subject to effective judgements.

For intellectual property-related criminal cases of second instance, the local people's courts accepted 787, more or less the same as the previous year; 812 cases were concluded, representing an increase of 3.83%.

In 2016, high profile criminal intellectual property cases heard by the people's courts include: a case of trade secret infringement by Wang Ziping; a case of counterfeiting registered trademarks by Shen Liang *et al.*; a case of counterfeiting registered trademarks and selling goods bearing counterfeited registered trademarks by Deng Fengcheng, Cheng Xianrong *et al.*; and a case of trade secret infringement by Peng Fan.

In 2016, the people's courts' adjudication of intellectual property cases presented the following four new features:

Highest ever number of cases: In 2016, the number of civil, administrative and criminal intellectual property cases accepted by the people's courts increased substantially. Of all the cases accepted, 152,072 were first instance cases, representing a 16.80% increase from 2015. Civil cases of first instance increased most substantially, by 24.82%.

In terms of geographical distribution, caseloads have remained high in five provinces and cities, including Beijing, Shanghai, Jiangsu, Zhejiang and Guangdong, where 107,011 intellectual property cases were newly accepted, accounting for 70.37% of the country's total. In Guangdong and Shanghai, newly accepted cases increased by 22.36% and 20.74% respectively. The caseloads for both Shandong and Fujian have increased by more than 20%. Other provinces where caseload was relatively low in previous years also witnessed big increases. For instance, due to advancing industrialisation and urbanization, case number in Guizhou grew sharply by 58.20% compared with the previous year. In Chongqing, the courts also witnessed a surge in the number of intellectual property cases accepted, which grew 57.85% from last year. In Hunan and Anhui, first instance intellectual property cases also increased rapidly, up by 52.02% and 45.4% respectively compared to last year.

Increasingly challenges in adjudication: Fact-finding for intellectual property cases, especially technology-related cases, involve complicated technical facts, and hearing such cases pose huge challenges. 2016 saw a significant increase in patent cases involving state-of-the-art technology, joint development of new technologies or application of technological outcomes. This has undoubtedly pose added challenges in terms of fact-finding and the analysis and judging of a case.

In 2016, courts in Shandong recorded a 119% year-on-year increases in cases relating to technology contracts. Of all the first instance cases concluded by the Shanghai Intellectual Property Court, more than

95% were technology-related disputes involving patents, computer software and technological secrets. The Beijing courts concluded a case of administrative dispute, where it invalidated "a nucleotide analogue compound or salt and its synthesis method" inventive patent involving complex pharmaceutical and chemical matters such as the Markush-type claim.

In addition to technology-related cases, there were trademark disputes relating to brand equity protection of well-known companies, copyright disputes involving new internet technologies, and monopoly and unfair competition cases concerning the preservation of market order. These are high-profile cases involving complicated and difficult facts, and required unusual approaches when applying the law, presenting new challenges to intellectual property adjudication. For instance, the "xiaolong" trademark opposition review case heard by Beijing courts involving the FC-1 Xiaolong fighter; Tencent's *The Palace: Lost Daughter* (*gong suo lian cheng*) copyright dispute involving interpretation of the right to transmit works over information networks; and Qihoo 360 and Baidu's unfair competition dispute involving Robots.txt protocol.

Consistent and improving quality and efficiency in adjudication: First, the percentage of reopened cases has declined significantly. In 2016, despite a 30.09% increase in concluded civil intellectual property cases of first instance, the rate of reversal of decisions and remanding for retrial at the second instance was 5.94%, almost unchanged from last year. Reopening rate has decreased by 45%, and the rate of administrative cases reversed and remanded for retrial at the second instance was 13.85%, representing a 1.56% decrease from the previous year.

Second, the post-mediation discontinuance rate has increased substantially. The local people's courts recorded a 64.21% post-mediation discontinuance rate for first instance cases and 27.44% for second instance cases, and the figures represent achievement of positive social and legal effects. In Shanghai's courts, 73.92% of civil intellectual property cases were discontinued after mediation. In Shandong Province, the rate of discontinuance after mediation for civil intellectual property cases of first instance reached 69.70%. In Tianjin Municipality, through coordinated efforts between the three levels of courts and by engaging in judicial activism and clear fact-finding, the several hundred copyright disputes relating to artist Qi Baishi's works were successfully mediated. Such mediation has enabled relevant parties to resolve their disputes that have been simmering for decades. Having designed innovative mediation methods, the courts in Jiangxi Province have facilitated the signing of copyright licensing agreements between more than twenty entertainment companies with collective management organizations. This has helped defuse social tensions and helped regulate the copyright market and reduce social costs.

Third, the number of concluded cases grew significantly. In Chongqing Municipality, the number of concluded intellectual property cases of first and second instances increased 62.74% from 2015; in Hunan Province, concluded first instance intellectual property cases grew by 48.79%; in Guangdong Province, concluded intellectual property cases increased by 42.82%; and in Jiangsu Province, concluded first instance intellectual property cases increased by 30.8% from last year.

Increased the amount of damages awarded: The People's Courts have been experimenting with using market value as the benchmark for determining damages in intellectual property cases, and have increased the protection of critical core technologies and well-known brands according to law. With the attorney's fee and other reasonable litigation costs properly factored in and punitive damages imposed when necessary, the quantum of damages was set to correspond with the market value of intellectual property.

In *Panasonic Corporation v. Zhuhai East Kingdom Electrical Appliance Co., Ltd*. and *Beijing Likang Fuya Trading Co., Ltd.*, an appellate case of design patent infringement, the Beijing High People's Court ruled in favour of Panasonic Corporation's full claim for damages worth 3 million yuan. In another two appellate cases involving the "*ziyu*" trademark infringement and repeat copyright infringement by Sursen Digital Technology Co., Ltd, the Beijing Intellectual Property Court also found in favour of the intellectual property owners' claim for full damages.

At the same time, the People's Courts have severely punished bad faith behaviour during litigation. Procedural or substantive sanctions were imposed according to law against such acts as falsifying evidence, misrepresentation, deliberately delaying production of evidence beyond the time limit, destroying evidence, or witness tampering. In a patent infringement case involving the Qingdao CO-NELE Machinery Co., Ltd as the plaintiff, the Beijing High People's Court imposed a 500,000-yuan fine on the party that refused to obey the court's preservation order that became effective.

II. Advancing judicial reform to improve the adjudication system

2016 marks the beginning of the 13th Five Year Plan period. It is also a breakthrough year for the People's Courts in terms of comprehensive deepening of judicial reform. Committed to the reform agenda and determined to break new grounds, the People's Courts have taken targeted measures to further revamp the judicial systems and mechanisms, and to modernise the intellectual property protection regime and capacity.

(1) Promoting the development of intellectual property courts

In 2016, intellectual property courts in Beijing, Shanghai and Guangzhou have carried out their work systematically and fulfilled their judicial functions effectively. Their judges have acted in concert and leveraged technological and systemic innovation to enable more professional, detailed and law-based practice. As the reform measures continued to produce positive and exemplary effects, the intellectual property courts saw growing credibility and international influence, portraying a new image for China's intellectual property protection regime. The intellectual property courts took the lead in initiating certain judicial reforms, such as having the chief justice and division chiefs hear cases regularly, changing the adjudication committee's functions, and exploring different ways for the adjudication committee to hear cases. The results of such initiatives were encouraging.

In 2016, the total number of civil and administrative intellectual property cases accepted by the above three intellectual property courts was 17,268 cases, among which 14,896 were concluded. Clearance rate was 86.26%. The Beijing Intellectual Property Court advanced the development of its case guidance research base; the Shanghai Intellectual Property Court has help in the development of Shanghai into a technological innovation hub; and the Guangzhou Intellectual Property Court has engaged in vigorous research in market-based operations of intellectual property. These are efforts that provide a new facelift for China's intellectual property adjudication practice.

The Intellectual Property Division of the Supreme People's Court delved into the difficulties and problems of the intellectual property courts' reforms and development and completed a report entitled "Establishing Intellectual Property Courts and Their Work Progress". SPC's Intellectual Property Division also conducted studies for its research project entitled "Major Issues in the Establishment of Intellectual Property Courts" to provide practical guidance to improve the intellectual property appeal mechanism.

(2) Intensifying the "three-in-one" adjudication reform

2016 saw major progress and breakthroughs in the "three-in-one" adjudication of intellectual property cases. Other than the intellectual property courts, the "three-in-one" operation, which combines the adjudication of civil, administrative and criminal matters, has been launched in all other People's Courts.

On 5 July, the "Opinions on Implementing the 'Three-in-One' Adjudication of Intellectual Property-Related Civil, Administrative and Criminal Cases at the National Level" was issued. On 7 July, the Supreme People's Court convened a meeting in Nanjing of Jiangsu Province to plan and roll out the "three-in-one" operation nationwide. "Three-in-one" adjudication has since taken on a new dimension.

Currently, the Supreme People's Court is communicating with the relevant departments on the prosecution of intellectual property crimes so that the relevant documents could be jointly issued at an early date to advance "three-in-one" adjudication. This will improve the judiciary's overall effectiveness in intellectual property protection.

(3) Setting up specialised intellectual property adjudication organs

The Supreme People's Court drafted the plan for establishing specialised intellectual property adjudication organs in Nanjing, Jiangsu, Wuhan and Chengdu and their jurisdictions. In early 2017, the above organs were established and began accepting cases. The Nanjing Intellectual Property Division and Suzhou Intellectual Property Division were respectively established under the Nanjing Intermediate People's Court and the Suzhou Intermediate People's Court. Each division will operate independently, and will exercise, within the province, cross-regional jurisdiction over patent and technology-related first instance civil cases. The Intellectual Property Division in Wuhan has adopted the "three-in-one" model and has jurisdiction for civil, administrative and criminal intellectual property cases in Wuhan, and patent and technology-related first instance civil and administrative cases in Hubei Province. Chengdu court's Intellectual Property Division exercises cross-regional jurisdiction within Sichuan Province for patent and technology-related first instance civil and administrative cases.

(4) Refining the fact-finding mechanism for technical facts

A sound technical fact-finding mechanism is essential for ensuring fair adjudication in intellectual property cases.

The Intellectual Property Division of the Supreme People's Court has issued the "Provisional Regulations on Several Issues Concerning Technical Investigation Officers of Intellectual Property Courts Participating in Litigation Activities", and is currently working diligently to develop guidelines for the selection and appointment of technical investigation officers.

The Shanghai High People's Court has formulated the "Guidelines on Forensic Examination of Technical Facts in Civil Intellectual Property Litigations", and has improved the multiple mechanisms for technical fact finding.

The Beijing Intellectual Property Court has set up a Technical Investigation Office and formulated "Administration Rules for Technical Investigation Officers". In 2016, the court's number of concluded cases relative to the number of case accepted increased by 27.5% over the previous year.

The Guangzhou Intellectual Property Court organised a technical expert advisory committee consisting of 29 experts from administrative organs, universities and research institutes to provide professional inputs on the court's adjudication work. In 2016, the court heard 88 cases that relied on technical experts or technical investigation officers, and the rate of post-mediation discontinuance of action was 64.7%.

The Guizhou Province High People's Court cooperated with Guizhou Provincial Department of Science and Technology to appoint science and technical experts to advise the court on cases involving specialised technical knowledge to ascertain the technical facts during fact-finding.

The Sichuan Province High People's Court has selected experts from such areas as electronic information technology, mechanical manufacturing, medicine, and new plant varieties and formed a roster of technical experts on intellectual property to buttress its technical fact-finding system.

(5) Improving the alternative dispute resolution mechanism

Increasing intellectual property caseload has put the People's Courts resources under severe strain. A stronger and better ADR mechanism is of practical importance for the judiciary to deliver quality and efficiency in intellectual property protection.

The Beijing courts have strengthened coordination with organizations such as the Beijing Intellectual Property Reporting and Complaints Centre and the Internet Society of China's Mediation Centre. They have mobilized administrative organs, industry associations and civil society organizations in resolving disputes resolution through conciliation.

The Shanghai Intellectual Property Court has established cooperation with ten social organizations and institutes, such as the Mediation Centre of the Internet Society of China, Shanghai Software Industry Association, Shanghai Biopharmaceutics Industry Association, the Civil and Commercial Mediation Committee of Shanghai Federation of Industry and Commerce, and Shanghai Oriental Notary Public Office. Together, they set up ADR cooperation mechanisms and aligned the litigation and non-litigation processes. By complementing each other and sharing resources within the ADR system, the court and its partners have promoted pre-trial mediation and aligned the litigation and mediation processes. In 2016, the Shanghai Intellectual Property Court referred 96 cases for pre-trial mediation with the parties' consent, and successfully mediated 23 cases.

By leveraging the advantages of industry associations and scientific and technical experts, the courts in Fujian Province have implemented mediation by appointment of the court, or by industry associations and technical experts. This allows the strengths of different channels to be synergised, and in turn, a large number of intellectual property disputes to be fairly and effectively resolved.

III. Strengthening supervision and guidance to unify standards for judicial decisions

Unifying decisions through harmonised standards provides fundamental value in improving the judiciary's credibility and authority. In 2016, the People's Courts continued to strengthen their work in terms of issuing judicial interpretations and developing judicial policies, and improved the work mechanisms for adjudication supervision and management. Also, much effort was dedicated to elevating the standard of adjudication of intellectual property disputes and to ensuring uniformity in judicial decisions.

(1) Strengthening judicial interpretation and judicial policies

Formulation of the "Supreme People's Court's Interpretation (II) of Issues Regarding the Application of the Law When Adjudicating Patent Infringement Disputes": Approved by the Supreme People's Court's Adjudication Committee on 25 January 2016 and effective on 1 April 2016, the Supreme People's Court's judicial interpretation provides clarity on application of the law pertaining to matters such as determination of patent infringement, choice and interpretation of patent claim, similar designs, indirect infringement, conflicting application defence, standard application defence, production or business purposes, lawful source (innocent infringer) defence, computation of damages, and application of Article 47 of the Patent Law, and will effectively enable the correct application of the Patent Law.

Formulation of the "Supreme People's Court's Regulations on Issues Regarding Adjudication of the Granting and Validation of Trademark Rights": Based on the Supreme People's Court's "Opinions on Issues Regarding the Granting and Validation of Trademark Rights in Administrative Disputes", and approved by validation's Adjudication Committee on 12 December 2016 and effective on 1 March 2016, the regulations aim at addressing salient problems in judicial practice by detailing the approaches in dealing with the key problems in granting and validating trademark rights for administrative cases and the practical difficulties encountered during adjudication. The regulations cover substantive aspects such as scope of examination, determination of distinctiveness, protection of well-known marks, and protection of the prior rights of copyright and right of personal name, and procedural matters such as violation of statutory procedure and *ne bis in idem*. Essentially, they embody the Supreme People's Court's practical experience in adjudication and in improving the standard in application of law in the granting and validating trademark rights, and hold great significance in respect of the judiciary's efforts in inculcating the notion of honesty and integrity, in developing a good discipline in trademark application and registration, and in unifying adjudication standards.

Formulation of the "Outline of the Judicial Protection of Intellectual Property in China（2016-2020）": Divided into seven sections, namely "Foreword", "Achievements", "Guiding Concepts", "Fundamental Principles", "Key Objectives", "Key Measures" and "Concluding Remarks", the outline is exposits the guiding tenets and objectives of intellectual property protection for the People's Courts in the next five years, defines the principles and measures with regard to protection, and sets forth the development roadmap and blueprint. It also plugs gaps by setting forth the direction and solutions to address the bottlenecks of judicial practice, thereby ensuring healthy development. This outline is the first of its kind targeting at a specific area of adjudication and issued by the Supreme People's Court. It is a measure that reflects the steps which the Supreme People's Court has taken to implement the Party Central Committee's core values, and embodies the Supreme People's Court's efforts to strengthen property protection and incorporate new concepts of economic development in the judicial protection of intellectual property. It is also an important outcome of the Supreme People's Court's fulfilment of the spirit of President Xi Jinping's important addresses, and its use of President Xi's new concepts, thoughts and strategies in governance and administration to provide direction for the judicial protection of intellectual property. The outline was released during National Intellectual Property Week in celebration of the "26 April World Intellectual Property Day".

The Supreme People's Court has also stepped up efforts in studying the "Supreme People's Court's Interpretation of Issues Regarding the Application of law Pertaining to Matters on Preservation during Adjudication of Intellectual Property and Competition Disputes" and "Supreme People's Court's Opinions on Issues Relating to Leveraging the Leading Role of Judicial Protection of Intellectual Property to Accelerate Development of an Intellectual Property Power". By improving judicial interpretations and judicial policies, the Supreme People's Court could better supervise and guide the courts in the protection of intellectual property.

(2) Strengthening adjudication guidance and research study

Drafting and revision of laws: The courts have actively participated in the drafting ad revision of various laws and regulations, including the Civil Code, Patent Law, Copyright Law, Anti-Monopoly Law, Seed Law, Rules of Implementation of the Trademark Law, provided inputs for their revisions, and recommended incorporation of intellectual property laws in the Civil Code. To study the amendment of the Patent Law, the Supreme People's Court has formed a special inter-agency research team to study and review systematically the implementation outcomes of the Patent Law. The Supreme People's Court drew on its experience of thirty years and examined in-depth the difficulties and problems relating to adjudication of patent disputes, and submitted to the

State Council Legislative Affairs Office general recommendations and recommendations on amendment of specific provisions.

Thematic studies on application of law:

Many courts have initiated thematic studies to strengthen capacity in the application of law.

Supreme People's Court: Organised a research study on "guidelines on intellectual property protection of business models and other new forms of innovative outcomes" to analyse the issues on the application of law during adjudication of civil disputes relating to movies and works created using methods similar to movie production, and the copyright collective management the system; worked with All-China Federation of Industry and Commerce to initiate a special study on intellectual property protection of private enterprises; participated in the crackdown of "headline-flagging gangs (*biaotidang*)" (i.e. using an alarming and unrelated title to an article to attract attention) to provide legal support in cleaning up the internet environment.

Beijing High People's Court: Conducted research studies and published the "Beijing High People's Court's Manual on Adjudication of Cases Involving Cyber infringement of Intellectual Property", which provided questions and answers on adjudication of cases relating to the granting and validation of trademark and patent rights.

Shanghai High People's Court: Conducted studies on "legal issues relating to multiple licensing of trademarks", "copyright infringement involving deep linking" and "protection of computer software patents".

Jiangsu Province High People's Court: Conducted study on "possible legal issues relating to supply-side structural reform and the judicial responses"; completed research reports as the "Research Report on Issues Relating to Adjudication of Cases Involving Trademark Infringement Disputes" and "Adjudication Criteria for Patent Cases under the Context of Technological Innovation".

Hunan Province High People's Court: Completed key soft science research relating to intellectual property rights, such as the "Study of the Discovery Mechanism for Technological Facts in Intellectual Property Cases" and "Study on the Conflict and Coordination of the Administrative Protection and Judicial Protection of Intellectual Property".

Guizhou Province High People's Court: Completed research report on "Intellectual Property Protection of Guizhou Tea: Models, Issues and Strategies" and key research topic "Protection of Intangible Cultural Heritage".

Jilin Province High People' Court: Conducted studies on Korean (Chosun) medicine and drugs to facilitate protection of TCM intellectual property.

Communicating and sharing with administrative agencies:

Supreme People's Court: Conducted operational exchanges with the Patent Re-examination Board (PRB) of the State Intellectual Property Office (SIPO) to further clarify and unify the laws and regulations pertaining to granting and validating rights; organised operational exchanges with the Chinese Trademark Review and Adjudication Board (TRAB) and held in-depth discussions on the application of laws relating to trademark protection; initiated with the Bureau of Seed Management, Ministry of Agriculture, a joint-study on the revision of the judicial interpretation of protection of new plant varieties.

Beijing High People's Court: Held seminars with the State Administration of Industry and Commerce's (SAIC) Trademark Office, TRAB and SIPO's PRB to discuss specific issues relating to application of law.

Inner Mongolia High People's Court: Communicated and coordinated with the cultural market administration authorities to resolve the series of cases involving copyright infringement by Karaoke operators, and has preliminarily put together a three-tier copyright royalty tariff for the Huhhot Municipality.

Using cases to guide adjudication: The Intellectual Property Division of the Supreme People's Court publishes representative cases (*dianxing anli*) regularly, and also prepares and issues "Adjudication Guidelines for Intellectual Property Disputes" and the "Annotated Intellectual Property

Guiding Cases". It issued its 16th set of guiding cases, among which is the *Qihoo 360 vs. Tencent* case on abuse of dominant market position, which was published on 6 March 2017. The Supreme People's Court's case guidance and research (Beijing) base reviewed the case guidance practice and initiated the relevant research studies.

IV. Implementing open justice to create a law–based environment that conduces to judicial protection

"Justice must not only be realised, but be tangibly realised." In 2016, the People's Courts have intensified efforts in promoting open justice by focusing on developing "sunshine justice" typified by open, dynamic, transparent and user-friendly features. By facilitating the transformation and upgrading of the open justice system, the courts hope to enable a more regulated, effective, sensitive and balanced system.

(1) Strengthening open justice to promote fair trial

Open court for major cases: During the "26 April World Intellectual Property Day" outreach period, the Supreme People's Court heard the *Michael Jeffrey Jordan vs. TRAB and Qiaodan Sports* Co. Ltd. case in an open court, the presiding judge of which was Vice President Tao Kaiyuan. Hearing and decision was broadcasted live in all media and the court proceedings were observed by diplomats from the United States, European Union, Japan and Korea, as well as representatives from the US Chamber of Commerce. Xinhua News, China Central Television (CCTV) and Singapore's Lianhe Zaobao were among the more than two dozen local and foreign media companies that sent their journalists to observe the entire proceeding, which was seamlessly delivered in real time on www.chinacourt.cn and the Supreme People's Court's official microblog Sina Weibo. The Supreme People's Court's Sina Weibo alone recorded more than 1.5 million viewings of the full live broadcast, with a total exposure of more than 98 million times. Open hearing of the case demonstrates to the world the openness and transparency of China's courts, and the good practice of fair justice and equal protection of the lawful rights of both local and foreign parties.

Ensuring public availability of written rulings and judgements: The People's Courts have continued to improve the management of online publication of written rulings and decisions, such that those suitable for making public will be promptly uploaded online for public supervision. Openness engenders fairness, and the people will truly feel equity and justice delivered by the judicial system.

Continued efforts in promoting open court proceedings: The courts promoted open court proceedings by promptly uploading case proceedings information onto the China Judicial Process Information

Online to ensure protection of the parties and the people's right of knowledge and right of supervision.

(2) Strengthening exchanges and cooperation to improve the image of the judiciary

By using the China International Exchanges (Shanghai) Base for Judicial Protection of Intellectual Property Rights as platform, the Supreme People's Court built a more robust international and regional exchange mechanism for judicial protection of intellectual property, and strengthened exchanges and cooperation with international organizations and other countries. Representatives from the courts participated in the U.S.-China Rule of Law Dialogue, working group meetings under the EU-China IP Dialogue mechanism, free trade agreements intellectual property chapter negotiations. The representatives also participated in various work group meetings involving foreign counterparts, such as the China-Switzerland, China-U.S., China-Australia, and China-Russia intellectual property work group meetings, and submitted written recommendations. Representatives were sent to the United States and Europe for study visits. The Supreme People's Court representatives also participated in the Seminar on "Enforcement of Plant Breeders' Rights under the UPOV Convention" organised by Hanoi, Vietnam, and the Briefing on China's Intellectual Property Protection regime organised by Korea.

The Shanghai High People's Court organised a successful EU-China Judges' Forum on "Innovation-Driven Economy and Intellectual Property Judicial Protection". This pre-eminent international meeting was well-participated by officials from more than a dozen countries, regions and international organizations, personnel from judicial authorities, and business representatives.

The Chongqing High People's Court and the Southwest University of Political Science and Law jointly organised several "China Intellectual Property Judges' Forum". The Shanghai High People's Court collaborated with the East China University of Political Science and Law and Tongji University to jointly establish a cooperation mechanism, and worked with the Shanghai University of International Business and Economics and the Shanghai University of Political Science and Law to set up a legal services volunteer mechanism.

(3) Broadening outreach channels to facilitate regular publicity activities

The intellectual property outreach week organised by the Supreme People's Court in celebration of the "26 April World Intellectual Property Day" has become a regular feature in IP judicial publicity. Other publicity activities include the "Judicial Protection for Intellectual Property: Wayfaring in Zhejiang" activity for central-level media, media briefing and press conferences, white paper on "Judicial Protection of Intellectual

Property Rights in Chinese Courts (2015)", the "Ten Major Intellectual Property Cases" and "Fifty Representative Intellectual Property Cases" adjudicated by Chinese Courts in 2015, and the "Supreme People's Court Annual Report (2015) on Intellectual Property Case".

Local courts also worked hard at expanding their publicity channels for effective publicity.

The Jiangsu Province High People's Court set up the "Intellectual Property Horizons" column in its Sina Weibo microblog account and a WeChat Public Account as platforms to communicate and review their experience in adjudicating major and challenging intellectual property cases.

The Jiangsu Province High People's Court created a section called "IP Convergence (*zhi zhi hui*)" in its website (www.zjcourt.cn) for sharing of intellectual property-related information. Viewership for the year exceeded 190,000 hits.

The Guangdong Province High People's Court requires that for cases to be eligible for participation in the "Outstanding Trial" award, hearing must be broadcasted live online. For cases that attract public concern, such QVOD Technology Co., a video-streaming website operating under Chinese name "Kuai Bo" involving the imposition of administrative sanction, and "If You Are the One (*fei cheng wu rao*)" TV dating show involving trademark infringement dispute, hearing was delivered in real time on the court's website.

To improve communication, the Shanghai Intellectual Property Court created a Chinese/English bilingual website and an official microblog and WeChat public account, accepted media interviews, and published 156 articles on media publications, such in Xinhua News and CCTV.

The Shaanxi Province High People's Court broadcasted five cases live and announced its decision for all five cases during the 26 April IP Outreach Week. They are cases of a new genre that have attracted public concern and that are representative and challenging. The activity was reported in Xi'an Daily and the People's Court Daily.

V. Strengthening people development to improve the overall quality of the adjudication team

People development provides the basis and assurance in judicial protection of intellectual property. The courts must fully appreciate the Party and the country's overall circumstances and the resulting new demands on people development in the intellectual property adjudication team. As such, they must observe strict discipline in party governance and follow the requirements under the "Opinions on Strengthening Development of Political and Legal Personnel under the New

Circumstances" to build an IP adjudication team that is steadfast in belief, that delivers justice for the people, that takes full accountability in their work, and that is clean and uncorrupted.

(1) Strengthening formation of ideological and political thoughts to elevate political calibre

People development for the intellectual property adjudication team has always followed the Party's leadership and focused on honing the "four consciousness (*sige yishi*)" (i.e. consciousness in terms of strengthening political integrity, employing a broad perspective, upholding the core leadership, and ensuring alignment with the Party and country's direction). It also meant learning and following through the spirit of President Xi Jinping's key addresses, adhering to the China-specific socialist rule of law approach, such that our minds, our political ideology and our actions highly aligned with the Party Central with comrade Xi Jinping as the core leadership.

Other important efforts are the "two learning and one being (*liangxue yizuo*)" activity where learning involves studying the Party's constitution and rules and the series of key addresses, and being involves becoming a qualified Community Party member; acquiring moral and humanist qualities from the excellent Chinese tradition and culture; upholding the advanced principles of socialism and the sound tradition of people-based justice; and voluntarily practising and stalwartly safeguarding the core value system of socialism.

(2) Strengthening the ability to discharge duties so as to elevate professional capabilities

Improving the ability to perform duties is an important people development goal for the intellectual property adjudication team. Thus, development of such ability must be substantially strengthened for continued improvement of adjudication quality. Development also aims to produce a huge pool of IP judges with macro perspective and has an international outlook, and who know the law, has the skills, and who possess inter-disciplinary knowledge, thereby enabling them adapt to the new era where knowledge is renewed and judicial practice develops rapidly.

The Supreme People's Court organised a national training for intellectual property judges, during which Vice President Tao Kaiyuan gave a special lecture. The local courts also organised many activities. To broaden training possibilities the Beijing High People's Court combined its annual training and seminar. The Beijing Intellectual Property Court organised different types of sharing sessions for senior judges to train and transfer their experience to younger judges. The Shanghai High People's Court held the "Legal Economics Advanced Level Seminar" and the "Legal Economics and Anti-Monopoly Advanced Level Seminar" to improve the judges' theoretical knowledge and professional capabilities. The Anhui

Province High People's Court included its new operational rules and new adjudication concepts into its group learning curriculum, and used its department WeChat group to expand its learning platform beyond the official "eight hours". The Hainan Province High People's Court proposed the "one main theme, two integrations, three forms of party branch, four consciousness, five major developments, and six principles (*yitiao zhuxian, liangge jiehe, sanxing dangzhibu, sizhong yishi, wuda fazhan, liuge yuanze*)" work methodology to integrate and advance the various aspects of work.

(3) Strengthening development of the judiciary's behaviour to create a good image

To forge iron, one needs a strong hammer. A strong team begets a flourishing undertaking; therefore, building a clean judiciary is integral to people development.

All our courts must ensure that they deal with both the symptom and the cause, and must delve deep when nurturing a good party ethos and clean administration and fight corruption. They must adhere to a stringent standard in education, management and supervision, and employ a zero-tolerance policy in punishing judicial corruption to ensure fair and clean justice.

At the individual level, the courts have strengthened people development by honing political character to build loyalty to the Party, by developing strict self-discipline, and by facilitating the drawing of lessons from cases involving violation of law and discipline. In doing so, any inclination of wrongdoing could be discover in time and further mistakes prevented. Also, by educating family members to create a family ethos of honesty and emphasising use of family bonding to strengthen anti-corruption measures, family members could become "gatekeepers" for the adjudication team.

Conclusion

2017 is an important year for implementing the 13th Five Year Plan. It is also a deciding year for furthering reform of the judicial system, and a year which judicial protection of intellectual property makes big strides in development.

Judicial protection of intellectual property by the People's Courts will follow through the spirit of President Xi Jinping's important addresses and his new concepts, thoughts and strategies in governance and administration, and will capitalise on the historic opportunities brought forth by the new round of technological revolution, and adapt to the new changes in the international landscape and the new normal in economic development. They will cultivate the "four consciousness", and implement the National Intellectual Property Strategy fully, improve the system of property right protection, and protect property rights according to law. All the above efforts will be carried out in observance of the "five areas in one (*wuwei yiti*)" framework where the economy, politics, culture, society, and the environment are jointly reformed, the requirements of the "four comprehensive (*sige quanmian*)" strategy, and the development notion of "innovation, coordination, greenness, openness and sharing".

The courts will focus on achieving the goal of "working hard to ensure that the people perceive fairness and justice in every judicial case". They will abide by the tenets of justice for the people and fair justice, leverage the leading role of the courts in the protection intellectual property, and strengthen judicial protection of intellectual property. They will also create a good legal environment to support implementation of the national strategy of innovation-driven development, and provide strong judicial protection to build a global power in intellectual property and technology. Indeed, the courts will usher in the successful convening of the 19th National People's Congress of the Chinese Communist Party with their magnificent results.